SCORPIO
October 23–November 21

You cannot
shake hands
with a
clenched fist.

✧ Indira Gandhi ✧

GERANIUM

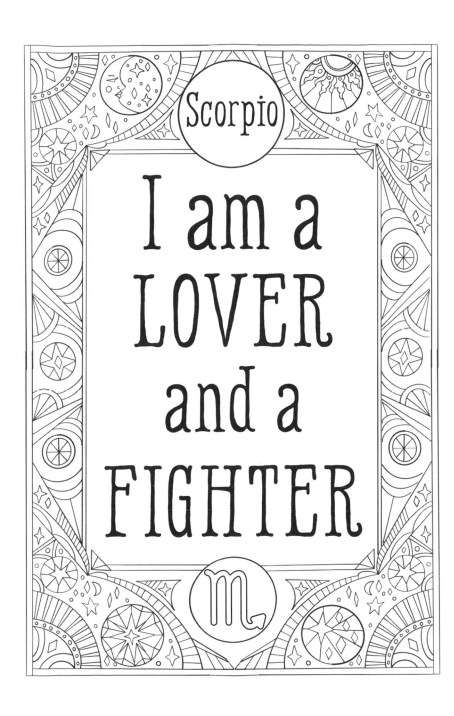

Scorpio

I am a LOVER and a FIGHTER

autumn

Scorpio

Never Underestimate a Scorpio

RULING HOUSE

8

The House of Rebirth

SCORPIO

◇

My vulnerability is my strength

◇◇◇

SCORPIO

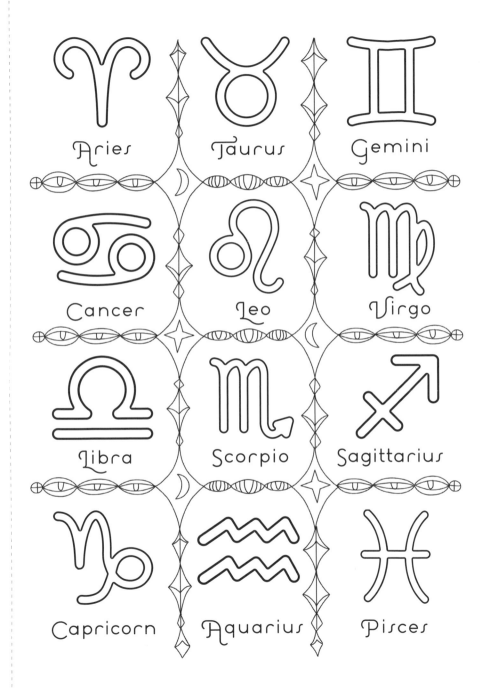

Aries Taurus Gemini

Cancer Leo Virgo

Libra Scorpio Sagittarius

Capricorn Aquarius Pisces

Water Signs

Cancer

Scorpio

Pisces

LET THE STARS LEAD THE WAY